DON'T FRET

(JAZZ POEMS)

BY

MICHAEL L. NEWELL

ACKNOWLEDGEMENTS

Most of these poems (sometimes in a somewhat different form) have appeared in the following publications, to whose editors grateful acknowledgement is made: *Bellowing Ark*; *Black Poppy Review*; *Current*; *Jerry Jazz Musician*; *Verse-Virtual*.

Some of these poems have appeared (some times in a different form) in the following books and chapbooks:

A Stranger to the Land	(Garden Street Press, 1997)
Collision Course	(Four-Sep Publications, 1999)
Meditation of an Old Man Standing on a Bridge	(Bellowing Ark Press, 2018)
Diddley-Bop-She-Bop	(Bellowing Ark Press, 2021)
Still the World Beckons: New and Selected Poems	(Cyber-wit.net, 2022)

I would like to tip my cap to the following editors who have treated my work kindly over the years and been most supportive in other ways as well: Robert R. Ward, Jerry Austin, Phil Wagner, Jack Hart, Don Wentworth, Firestone Feinberg, Christopher M., and Joe Maita.

I would also like to thank the following folk for their kindness to my work over a span of many years and for their generous friendship: Anna Citrino, Michael Citrino, David Ellenstein, Robert Fox, Joseph Glaser, Stellasue Lee, Michael Minassian, Lawrence Noel, Ed Ruzicka, and Robert Wexelblatt.

Cover artwork: Michael Citrino
Author Photo: Wendy Keller

ISBN: 978-93-95224-24-6
Tel: +(91) 9415091004 E-mail: info@cyberwit.net

E-mail: info Tel: +(91) 9415091004 @cyberwit.net

TABLE OF CONTENTS

This book is dedicated to Joe Maita who has published three-fourths of the poems in this book in his fine online magazine, *Jerry Jazz Musician.* His encouragement has led me to write a large percentage of the poems in this book. Without his generosity, many of these poems would never have come into existence. Keep on trucking, brother, keep on trucking. Your magazine is a beacon for many lovers of jazz.

AND SO JAZZ CAME TO BE

In the bible of jazz, ragtime (with its syncopated, ragged rhythm
set the rules of the musical landscape that grew into jazz),
      led to Dixieland (wild and wooly, and hot hot hot,
      and brothers and sisters, that's no jive, that is just
      staying alive with crazy beats)
            which begat swing (which was no small thing
            making the off-beat central and making melody
            lure lovers onto dance floors, where music made
            love to them, and they made love to one another),
    which brought forth bop (bop at the speed of sound,
    cool bop, hard bop, bop that rocked harder than rockers do,
    bop that rediscovered how melody and rhythm could interrelate),
            thence came free jazz where all sound is possible, rules are
            negotiable, nothing is knowable, all is doable,
            freedom, freedom, all can be found and done, oh yeah,
            let the listeners catch up on their own, don't stop and wait
            for them, let them take off the top of their heads and imbibe
            the music in great gulps and find the sense wherever
            or whatever it may be,
    then fusion arrived with its wild marriage of jazz, rock, blues,
    electronic experiments, melody cradled in rock guitars, drums
    almighty and newly freed, basses and pianos set loose to blend
    sounds and rhythms new to this world, trumpets and saxes
    let music loose that reminded listeners of times past while charting
    new and sometimes feral paths,
            and the future waits for the next unexpected paths to what
            jazz can be, will be, while never forgetting what it has been,
and thus jazz came to be, is, will be, ever and ever in the streets, clubs,
records, movies, and hearts of men and women uplifted and shifted
in what the world means to them, and we listen for what is new, and rejoice
in what has been and continues to be. Amen, brothers and sisters, Amen.

YOU ARE TOO BEAUTIFUL

The woman across the restaurant
smiled as she floated at her table,
while the juke box played, "You are

too beautiful and I am a fool for beauty."
The pianist painted a solo that lifted us both

to our feet where we met, swirled, embraced,
silently investigated all movement available
to our limited bodies, and then once again

Johnny Hartman pointed out your beauty
and my foolishness for beauty, as piano

faded away, percussionist drifted final notes
into distance, and you swayed to your seat while I
drifted to my table as Coltrane slowly seated me.

I wonder whether beauty so entrances due to perfection
of feature or due to imagination of rapt beholder.

(For Johnny Hartman and John Coltrane)

THE CONCERT HAS ENDED

It was over, all done, trees chopped, nuts cracked,
the bass swayed and wandered off stage into a forest,
with a soft, steady, thump, thump, thump; trumpet

lifted off, aloft crooning a rising tune in search

of some moon or another; sax relaxed into series

of screeches, scratches, whooshing hither and thither,
cloud-borne, and the wind grown reedy; drums
tapping their way home down dark, empty, chilly streets;

piano lifting off, and thudding back to earth, lifting off,
and twisting and spinning through a windstorm of rising
and falling notes, it splashes down into a river whose current

is wilder than the wilderness of notes indigenous to the piano;

over time all grows silent, not an instrument can be heard;

only wind, cracking branches, and the steady tap tap tap
of some old fool loose in a midnight world rambling, ambling
toward some unknown destination, maybe even home.

SOME FREE FORM JAZZ

His name was unknown, unseen, unheard, kept solely to self,
      until someone named him Coleman, cold man,
perhaps a cool man, coalman, coals for man to be cool,
      cool man, hot to the touch, a colossal man,
a man clipped, clobbered, ta rara boom de ay,
      oh for some meaning, even meaning lost in wind,

in waves, in wandering currents of life, life, lost life,
      found life, life sputtering in chill, in ice,
in no meaning, in any meaning, in confusion, concussion,
      clarity, in whatever is manifest in the moment,
any moment, each moment, in whatever is momentous,
      so you see jazz be here, there,

and everywhere, just chop'em up words,
      chop'em up sounds, and put it all together, however
you feel like doing, throw in a bounce step, or three, or four,
      and you have a tune, a dance,
a wild, wet, and woolly song for life,
      your own jazz recital, homemade, and played just

this once.

FREE FORM JAZZ

my hat is having
another conversation
with the wind and rain

as my aged arms and legs
cavort in frivolous abandon
branches break loose and tumble

in wild improvisational designs up
and down a street bare of people where
all is frenetic motion tree bush abandoned

goats and chickens with water water everywhere
creating gullies all down the dirt road that mutate into
small creeks and ponds soon wind runs roughshod over all

Kigali, Rwanda, December 2012

IN ARCTIC REGIONS OF THE HEART

Bill Evans explores
"My Foolish Heart"
with the care of a mountain man
who treks through snowdrifts
in a frozen land of remarkable
beauty that nonetheless could
turn a traveler into a corpse

without anyone knowing it;
Chuck Israel's bass picks listeners'
feet up and puts them down,
guiding them safely through snowdrifts
of frozen emotion while the drums
of Larry Bunker feed heat to limbs
of listeners and of fellow musicians;

this trio swings effortlessly, yet exercises
a restraint that means no one is seared
by emotion, but everyone is aware
of beauty and danger side by side,
until at last music fades into rising
applause that warms musicians
and listeners with a sonic blanket.

LOST IN MUSIC OF A GENIUS

Cool, cool, ineffably cool,
his trumpet grieves with
a restraint barely able to be
embraced by listeners, his music
is pain on ice, whiskey frozen

on tongue and lips;
his song will be carried
to listeners' graves;
Miles has reached his resting place,
but his music which froze
heart and mind, allowed grief

to seep out slowly, still lives on
in audio and video; listeners
not alive when he died
listen and exude tears,
salt water that oozes into a world

of astonishing beauty that cares not
about us, yet sorrow and perfection
fill the world we see and the world
we hear from music left behind
by a flawed genius who knew beauty's
pain and pain's marriage to beauty.

For Miles Davis

LAD WITH BOTTLENECK GUITAR

The lad waiting for English class to start
always played slide guitar, improvising
melodies and inventing lyrics about
hunting and fishing, lyrics he never
finished and which often veered into
descriptions of female classmates,
some of whom would dare him to sing
about them, challenge inevitably accepted.

I would suggest he put the guitar away, but
classmates would beg for one more song,
always one more, a process that would
never end unless I turned into an ogre,
which would prompt one final partial song,
a bluesy lament about teachers who lacked
heart, who lacked love of music, and a final
line lamenting my inability to dance.

BEAUTY OF ENDINGS

sunset sprays horizon with burst
of color brilliant and striking
as Clark Terry solo soaring up and up
until its silvery virtuosic sheets
of sound reach stunning silence

GRIEF NOTES

sound of a midnight train
riding an autumn wind

a solo mountain fiddle
mourning its lost forest

a pennywhistle soaring
through a slow Irish air

a tenor sax breathing
the pain of back alleys

lonely bars a red light circling
a three a.m. fallen body

a mother's lullaby while walking
a sick infant all night long

and the hitchhiker humming Woody Guthrie
tunes alone on an empty highway

BROTHER WHERE ARE YOU

From nearby apartment, horn half-soars,
half-staggers, and a voice battered by years

half-talks, half-sings, "Brother Where Are You
They Told Me That You Came This Way;"

and I recall Oscar Brown Junior singing this song
on a college stage fifty-four years ago;

even now as two old men revisit words and melody
with less than perfect command of voice and horn,

I am moved, and I see across the years Brown
and his amazing band electrifying the audience;

I bless the old men on a porch doing what they
can do to make the song live decades later.

Once again music has tied my declining years to a time
when all was hope, and life was defined by song.

SAETA

a horn ripples with loss mourns
is joined by a rising drumbeat

trumpets join the song
choir of horns announces that

a funeral march approaches
solo trumpet breaks its heart upon life's rocks

march of the heart ensues that laments
and is martial simultaneously

trumpet seizes stage wails moans sobs
while drums slowly maintain heartbeat

all that is sorrow that mourns that grieves
fills the trumpet's sound

and the drum maintains the rhythm
of a funeral march while the trumpet

rises cracks its notes breaks its heart
upon life's stones all is loss loss loss

the drumbeat becomes regular and powerful
horns join the melody it too becomes regular

then fades to trumpet shadowed
by low voiced horn

drums become aural shadows
slowly dissolve into passing breeze

arrival of silence leaves life swaying on knife's point
and all grief lingers profoundly above still witnesses

night hovers in the distance
nothing will be the same again

      from *Sketches of Spain*

THERE ARE MANY TYPES OF REQUIEMS
(for David)

He was back only a few months from the Marines,
and a year in Vietnam playing funeral music
on his trumpet on land and at sea for deceased
servicemen.

Alone in his apartment, save
for a brother in another room, he played
his horn one last time, a slow mournful blues
shaped by a Harmon mute, a melody tear-filled
with loss, death, remembered laughter, and wild
shenanigans that drifted away into memory's vast
ecosystem.

For every loss, young men's offbeat humor
and unbridled playfulness attempted to fill the void.
The muted heart-wrenching melody infused with loss,
remembrance, and all that had been, filled the apartment
for thirty minutes or more. Then, in the middle
of a poignant phrase, the horn slid into silence.
The musician put down the trumpet, picked up
his motorcycle helmet, walked outside to his cycle,
and spent the next eight hours driving up and down
the Southern California coastline.

He never again played the trumpet.
Its fate was to slowly blacken on a closet shelf.

The solo witness has been haunted by what he heard
for a lifetime. Casualties of war come in many
shapes, sizes, and have an extensive range of causes.

Few wounds are worse than the loss of creating music.

ABANDONED BUT NOT FORGOTTEN

One of my greatest joys for decades
was exploring unknown record shops.
I once walked into a newly opened used
shop around the corner from my university
and discovered a used album, apparently
the improvisatory result of a session
set up by Norman Granz that included
Clark Terry, Dizzy Gillespie, Freddie
Hubbard, Oscar Peterson, Joe Pass,
Ray Brown, and Bobby Durham.
The album contained two (or maybe
three, I don't remember) LPs
that I played for years until I moved
abroad and gave the album away.
The store had a wonderful selection
of jazz, but closed within the year
which I found heartbreaking.

(continued on next page)

In Tallinn, Estonia, I was walking
down city streets in the middle
of a blinding snowstorm, stepped
into a small building that had several
small businesses in it, in order
to figure out where I was and how
to get back home, and found I was
standing next to a record shop
that carried new and used CDs,
all of which were jazz. I left there
with albums by Lee Morgan, Miles Davis
(from his later years), "A Love Supreme,"
"My Favorite Things," "Tokyo Blues,"
Milt Jackson, Sun Ra, and half a dozen
other albums. Over the next six months,
I returned there every couple of weeks.
Who would have thought such a shop
would be in the middle of a small building
in Estonia, and that I would find it in the middle
of a Sunday snowstorm? The old guy running
the shop knew more about jazz than most
musicians, and always seemed to have
whatever I (or anyone else) was searching for.

(continued on next page)

There was a little cassette tape shop in Abu Dhabi
that sold rip off copies of rock, jazz, blues, reggae,
classical, bluegrass, Celtic, and American folk music.
Such rip off shops were common throughout Abu Dhabi
in 1992, but this was the only place that seemed to have
whatever music one might desire. The little Syrian
proprietor seemed to be familiar with, and able to discuss,
virtually any type of music, and do so in Arabic, English,
French, Spanish, German, and Italian. He gave new meaning
to music being a universal language. He loved Jimi Hendrix,
Shania Twain, The Chieftains, Doc Watson, Bob Dylan,
Mozart, Bach, autoharp music, Bob Marley, Leadbelly,
and a host of other disparate musical artists.

In the not so distant past, there were such shops in London,
Los Angeles, Tallinn, Abu Dhabi, Amsterdam, Portland, Kuwait City,
and other cities in other countries around the world. Most of them
have faded into time, like a Bill Evans solo, or the final notes
sung of a Woody Guthrie song by Cisco Houston. Time swallows all.
Yet there are a few of us who still remember, and as long as
we remember, the musicians and record shops will hang in the air,
a slowly dissipating mist containing whispers of what once was
in the wisps of times past that ferry lost notes, fading voices,
and dreams of an unachievable future that wrap us round
in a quietly joyous melancholy that warms and elicits tears.

OXFORD STREET, LONDON, DECEMBER 2002

Clutter ruckus, confined
chaos, cracked coherence,
a boulevard bedazzlement
where bodies surge and swarm
in shifting patterns of confusion.

Salvation army bands, marching
and corner concert, fill the air
with Christmas tunes, a few feet
away a steel drum band plays
island versions of the same tunes.

A boy sits against a wall playing
French cafe music on a diatonic accordion,
hat on the ground, change fills the hat
and scatters beyond. People step over
and around the lad.

A cacophony of languages can be heard
babbling cheerfully away: Russian, Italian,
Polish, French, Swahili, Arabic, Spanish,
German, Japanese, Tagalog, and a pocketful
of other tongues from around the world--

now and again English is heard, often
in an accent which betrays the speaker
as being from elsewhere. Cars honk, buses
roar past, motorbikes zip between clogged lanes
of traffic, pedestrians dodge in and out.

A light changes, a wind
sweeps crowds across streets.
People scatter like autumn leaves,
reform into piles at next light. The clamor
(feet, horns, and voices) deepens,

reaches a climax, subsides
into silent streets of Christmas Day.

ONE EVENING WALKING IN LONDON DECEMBER 2002

Just off Oxnard Street (littered with last minute shoppers
two days before Christmas), an old man decked out
in a ragged trench coat and a torn stocking cap
played a slow mournful jazzy interpretation
of "Time after Time" on a battered flute.

The flute echoed through neighboring streets,
drawing a few pedestrians here, a few more there,
who joined a crowd that materialized from a nearby bookstore
and from a small eatery on the nearest corner.
The old guy never looked up, never acknowledged

the presence of anyone or anything other than the music
he was playing as he swayed side to side, back and forth,
and shuffled a few slow dance steps that were slurred in time
to certain notes he was bending. When he finished, one last
long phrase hanging in the chill night air, the crowd silent

and still, he gingerly slipped the flute into a deep coat pocket
and hobbled off, indifferent to slowly building applause rising
behind his back. As the crowd dispersed, a few voices
could be heard humming the tune; one or two knew the lyrics.
I sat down on a chair outside the bookstore and quietly laughed

at startling discoveries available in the most unexpected places,
and realized I was humming the tune and running my own
semi-musical riffs on the melody. A bookstore clerk leaving
for the night listened to me for a second, and tossed in a few notes
of his own improvising before vanishing into a suddenly empty night.

LISTENING TO SAYONARA BLUES

ripple them keys with the right hand Mr. Silver
while the left drones a steady beat beneath

it's near the end of the tune and the piano has taken over
and is musing about life about parting about loss

the drummer taps out exclamation points
the bass walks a straight line with a bounce and a hop

here come the horns singing about hope of life
round the corner just down the block next door

they know about pain wedded to joy
loss blended with a dram of the world's beauty

say goodbye to drudgery say goodbye to the ordinary
slip and slide side to side and say hello to the world

a new kind of sayonara a new kind of parting
where the future's promise dances alongside

THREE FOR PAOLO BURZESE

JAZZMAN

Breath across
reeds, rasps:

note evolving
into notes, a chain --

viral, geometric,
spiraling into constellations.

Open bedroom
windows -- SEE! HEAR!

Hope's hues
drape the living,

spread honey
to the hips.

EARLY MILES

Early Miles was all vowel,
a blue, black, ebony sweep,
the sound of life lived deeply
as a diver can dive into
bottomless water.

Bottomless the water
a diver can dive into,
the sound of life lived deeply,
a blue, black, ebony sweep,
early Miles was all vowel.

The sound of life lived deeply,
a blue, black, ebony sweep
a diver can dive into,
early Miles was all vowel,
bottomless the water.

A blue, black, ebony sweep,
early Miles was all vowel,
bottomless the water --
the sound of life lived deeply
a diver can dive into.

A diver can dive into
a blue, black, ebony sweep:
bottomless water, early Miles
was all vowel, the sound
of life lived deeply.

GETTIN' DOWN
                (after Paolo Burzese)

             "He let jazz curl
             a french horn around his knees."

His fingers, drumsticks, were
Buddy Rich, rat-a-tat, Philly Joe Jones, rat-tat-a-tat,
Max Roach, a-tat-a-tat

and his lips, slipped
into cymbals--all soft rhythm,
hissed promises of a night ahead, ah, but

his thoughts--all muted trumpet
and sax, sax, sax---mmm, baby!

Across the room she smiled, her wild
black hair the moan
of a slow trombone--

a two person quintet, they jammed
the night away.

FIRST SNOWSTORM OF THE YEAR

A feathery
buffeting

all day it swarmed
until our thoughts

were gusts of white
icy shavings

each flake an event
sculpted on air

jazzy mobiles
freeform and

cool as a Miles
Davis solo.

FIVE MINIATURES

my feet beat street
drummer just behind beat
where oh where is Philly Joe Jones

wind whispers song of grief
its version of
Ben Webster's sorrowful solos

Buddy Rich on drums
hands and arms ablaze
raises crowd in jubilation

every breeze every flower
every wild stream's power
nature's symphony

all day all night wind rain shake
house polyrhythmic dance
of roof walls floor
Elvin Jones thunders round us
gone he lives on in wild storm

SENOR BLUES, WHY IS YOUR OPUS DE FUNK?

Oh, Mister Silver, please please please,
don't make me beat my feet
no more no more no more.

I've been finger poppin', thinking
about Juicy Lucy, dreaming
of some sweet stuff,

wanting to come on home to some
home cookin', I've been hankerin'
to hear a song for my father,

I've been sighin' and cryin' because
my woman is so lonely that I've got
silver treads among my soul.

The preacher says I've got to stop
creepin' in to room 608, forget them Calcutta
cuties, lose those Tokyo blues,

cease and desist from swingin' the samba, stop
time, cool those restless natives in my heart
and soul, and find some peace peace peace.

for Mister Horace Silver

POWER OF RHYTHM

Let us begin by noting

drums ensnared by sticks
in hands of Buddy Rich;
flicks of his wrists generate

rhythmic melodies that lift

bodies to feet that create
dances unknown prior
to encountering the magic

in Rich's rich assortment

of rhythms leading listeners
to tap, bounce, swirl, twirl,
discover how bodies can

express life's manifold rhythms.

BUDDY RICH DRUM SOLO 1974

Buddy Rich launches into a solo,
hands dancing across drums, body
at first lethargic, all energy in hands
and arms, then a gradual build, more
and more of body involved, suddenly

cymbals join the dance, speed
and intensity sound like a jet taking off,
a wild conversation among drums erupts,
cymbals intrude briefly, and drums create
a marching martial rhythm which becomes

quieter and quieter, yet faster and faster,
drumsticks enter into dialogue with rims,
and gradually Rich rises in an explosive build,
nearly standing as drums and cymbals
all demand the listeners' unimpeded attention;

without warning his hitherto unnoticed big band bursts
into a powerful supporting swell of music,
and Rich explodes to a finish beyond what might
have been foreseen; drums and horns roar to mighty
finish that elicits a wild explosive clamor from the audience.

ALWAY THERE IS MUSIC

A wanderer, a gambler, a wild heart
who rambles up and down hills,
across valleys, he loves to drum

the land he crosses with his feet
beating out a heartbeat, at times
slow, other times rapid, but always

a beat beat beat that suggests
he bestows life through his feet
as he wanders thither, hither, round

and about, and always he sings
old songs he has known for decades;
he breathes music, he converses

through tunes, rhyme, and rhythm,
he defines life through music he hears,
shares, creates, repeats; he walks

with a lilt and bounce to his step; his
voice, singing, humming, speaking,
or whispering, always seems at one

with breeze, wind, falling water,
or thundering sky; all life, he says,
is music, and all music enriches life;

even when he snores while sleeping,
he sounds as though he were some old
singer such as Louis Armstrong, Clark Terry,

or even perhaps Son House or Howling Wolf;
the world entire is a cauldron bubbling music
music music; without it life is bereft.

MUSIC ALL OVER THE LAND

Wind winds its way through and round
stand of Douglas firs, escorting rain
to resting places, enriching land, bush,

tree, and plant, while wrapping a few lonely

figures drifting through landscape
in mist dampening bodies and cleansing minds,
creating a melancholy joy like a solo

by John Coltrane playing a slow ballad,

showing how the blues can embrace mind,
heart, and spirit in its quest for the perfect
tune, rhythm, and ineffable wilderness of notes.

AT AN NPR TINY DESK CONCERT

Golden soprano notes of Gary Burton's vibes are
embraced by baritone and alto notes of Chick Corea's piano,
as they float up to form a crystal architecture filled with sound

that creates a silence in heart and mind resonating
with beauty, hope, a landscape defining the paradox
of sophisticated sound clearing mind and heart

of life's impediments, leaving all senses open for whatever
may present itself, weaving dark and light, day and night
together forever, sound which creates a crystal silence where

listeners are entranced, and all is possibility, possibility, possibility.

UNEXPECTED

dawn snow flawless
as a Bill Evans solo
no birdcall no footprints
only an old fellow

crouched on his front porch
focused on hum of a breeze
through fir trees and solitary
cat motionless beneath bushes

the ancient breathes deeply
of autumn air and stares
fascinated at clouds floating from
his mouth when he breathes out

where he wonders is Stan Getz
to heat the world when you need him

ONE FOR BEN WEBSTER

I swing slowly on old wooden
seat attached to tree branch

no company but crows
decades of memories

and a breeze soloing
like a slithery breathy

tune such as Ben Webster
once whispered to a world

often inattentive but for those
who listened life grew richer

love more fulfilling and time
lasted forever or as long as he played

his sax blew notes perpetually lovely
perpetually blue his music an embrace

that made flesh and bones shiver
in delight and curved lips into smiles

COURTSHIP

Across dance floor she smiled;
her wild black hair was

moan of slow trombone;
his laughter was trumpet

seductively filtered
through Harmon mute;

and they glided into
one another's arms

embracing night
and the future.

JUST ANOTHER NIGHT AT THE CLUB

Every time the young airman drifted
into the club, he wandered over,
to the jukebox, slipped in a quarter,
and punched the button for "My Funny
Valentine," the fifteen minute version
featuring Miles Davis. He sat alone,
eating a tuna salad sandwich, slurping

a diet coke, swaying, humming,
imagining he was floating across
the dance floor with Angelita del Mundo,
the two of them alone with night
and one another. When music faded
to silence, another airman popped in
a quarter, and Jimmy Smith unleashed

"Got My Mojo Working." The young
dude got up from his seat and bopped
his way out the door, swinging, swaying,
singing along with Jimmy Smith,
whirling, twirling, spinning, grooving,
until he disappeared into the night.
Jimmy Smith's organ lit up the joint,

even though no more than four people
were present besides the bartender,
cook, and busboy, all of whom, although
they knew the music well, couldn't stop
high stepping, shoulder shaking, uttering
life affirming shouts, singing out of tune
with a joyous fervor, welcoming the night.

WHEN DOES THE MUSIC END

Five, five alive, young jazz musicians there were,
three men on sax, a woman on trumpet,
and a crazy girl in her teens making
drums explode in, out, and around
her compadres and an electrified audience;

two hours of free form exploration,
expression ranging from beat your feet
dance music to total chaos with mere
hints of organization to bare whispers
that would flower into wildly swaying

feathers of sound until at last silence,
silence that somehow continued to sing;
leaving the concert a friend turned to me,
asked whether I was coming; I smiled
and whispered, I'm going to listen to that

drummer for a while longer; my friend looked
around, asked are you sure; I put a finger
to my lips, whispered I think I am also going
to listen to the trumpet player carve some notes
through her Harmon mute, see where they take me;

my friend, perplexed, left me with ghosts
of sounds that swayed to and fro, while I
hummed improvisations, bounced, bopped,
and closed my eyes to see and hear better;
diddley-bop-she-bop does not begin to express that night.

LOOK AROUND THE BLUES ARE ALWAYS THERE

An old fellow sat on a park bench,
wind in his hair, wind billowing
through his clothes, as he blew
his flute, notes breeze-blown
across grassy fields, and through
rows of trees, the wind orchestrating

the tune which was new to him, found
in leaf-song and setting sun, a blues
improvised upon, to welcome the night
oncoming, which would envelop all passing,
turning them into shadow, as the ancient
chap faded; as I passed, I moved slowly,

so I could listen and watch as both man
and tune dissolved into the gloaming,
a whisper of a blues tune and a dimly
perceived shape; then the murmur
of a pond was all that was left, and I
discovered both my hands were barely visible,

and I strolled on into the night.

SCENES FROM THE CAFE
(Tashkent, Uzbekistan, Winter, 1999)

Talking near piano and wooden bar are three deep in conversation:
a Russian pianist who loves Simon and Garfunkel,
an Uzbek singer whose passions are
Sinatra, Bennett, and Chet Baker (he performs
their songs to taped accompaniment
in a sparsely filled backroom), and an American teacher
whose consuming interests are Celtic, Appalachian, Delta Blues,
Inca music, and Miles Davis. The three argue the relative
merits of melody and rhythm, music with lyrics
and music unadorned by language.

*

The tape deck wails with Turkish music.
An Irishman and a Kazakh, businessmen, share
a farewell meal. The Irishman keeps calling
for "The Rose of Tralee."

*

Young Russian and Ukrainian women belly dance to a tune
from a James Bond thriller while Turkish businessmen
stuff money down their skirts. A fiftyish expatriate, a ringer
for Sydney Greenstreet, works hard to impress a peroxide blonde.
A well-dressed professional couple slump in their seats, stare
into space with faces stripped of expression.

*

Midnight. One American customer and the staff (Russian, Uzbek,
Tajik, Estonian, and Korean) sip coffee, cola, wine, and listen
to Aretha Franklin ask for some R-E-S-P-E-C-T. Everyone sings along
and fakes a dance step or two. An old drunk outside
presses her face against the window and laughs. The staff takes a bow.

BACKWARD COUNTRY BOY BLUES

music insists move your feet
bip bop swing sway dance the night
away beyond human limitations
music is life brother life is movement
and all movement is a kind of dance

whoa daddy cut a rug darling slip and slide
fly hand over hand hip over hip
and the world comes alive in ways
just walking down the street can never
enlighten your body your soul your wild

freeborn heart and the piano sings
the bass strings legs into a whop bam
boom movement that can never be repeated
and the drum leads you to beat your feet
to swirl twirl and embrace as each takes

a turn flying through the air there ain't nothing
like these backward country boy blues
thanks to the dancing song of the Duke along
with Max and Mingus three who make life
an elegant embrace of space sound and time

lucky the listener who flings himself herself
into the musical arms of these three giants
and when the song ends when the dance floor
empties back into the night each who has spent
their time and hearts here will never my friend forget

(for Duke Ellington, Charles Mingus, and Max Roach)

JUST AN OLD JOINT

round midnight derelicts gather
in a coffee shop whose walls
are splintered whose roof long since
has lost the battle with wind and rain
floor littered with pans catching
water filtering through the roof
city rules are ignored and smoke
from cigarettes cigars and weed

create an indoor storm front
an old man in the corner quietly
plays jazz and blues tunes to which
he occasionally adds his ruined voice
no one pays much attention
the waitress who doubles as a cashier
and the cook who is the owner
make sure all have coffee food such

as it is will be delivered when they get
to it none of the customers give a damn
about when chow arrives they just need
a place out of the rain and wind and a few
like minded souls with whom they can chat
argue a place where if they are so inclined
they can nod off the joint will close
around two in the am until then they have

a moody haven where they can safely shelter
by two half of them will be asleep and will
need the owner and his waitress to shepherd
them all out the door last to leave is the old
guitarist who walks out still playing old blues tunes
nodding his head in his own world even as he
shambles out the door into a dark wet windy
wildly uncertain world made livable only by his music

AN AFTERNOON ALONE WITH THE WEATHER

Wind blends with rain all afternoon;

the sky is evening by noon,
and I croon out of tune with old

Nat King Cole and Bing Crosby songs
in a voice badly worn by time,
yet exuberant in accompanying music

from childhood, unleashing joy,

grateful to be alone, so I feel free
to unleash remnants of a voice

ragged as old trousers worn too long;
I eventually laugh at how ludicrous
this all would appear to a stranger,

and I create a drumbeat of laughter

that unleashes my feet in a clumsy
stutter step homemade dance; and rain

strokes window panes like drum brushes,
with an unexpected grace that makes
me whirl and lean out the window

to accept water's blessing on face and shoulders.

JAM SESSIONS ARE UBIQUITOUS

Rain dances on windowpanes,
flutters off glass, explores
wilderness of time and space,

as Milt Jackson's mallets sing
and swing on resonators, unleash
sound seducing bodies into movement;

listeners swerve and dance hither
and thither on either occasion:
all life a pretext for jazz.

TRIBUTE TO MODERN JAZZ QUARTET

Softly as in a morning sunrise,
Milt Jackson and John Lewis
make pianos and vibes dance
through imagined morning dream,

bright and stormy; audience hears,
sees brilliant raindrops swiftly dance
on waves, and double bass
in Heath's hands drives piano

and vibes in a wild, yet always
controlled dance; Connie Kay's
drums control from start to finish
the group's energy, drive, perpetual

life life life, a-swirl, a-blaze, and bass
is the heartbeat beat beat, as piano
and vibes explore what there is
in sky, water, land, and life, oh so lively

wild life which seeks more life, unquantifiable
life, and all sings, all swings, as the group climbs
musical stairs in search of the perfect sunrise,
the perfect morning, as they finally fade

into audience's wild, ecstatic, uninhibited applause
which will also drift off, as clouds do, as life does.
Outside the sun seeps through, painting clouds
with rainbow; soon rain and clouds drift into distance.

**DUKE ELLINGTON MAX ROACH CHARLES MINGUS SWING
SING**

bass opens the door
        drums enter
                piano strides authoritatively behind

chords crash
        courtesy of The Duke
                Mingus drives the trio along
                        drums unleashed by Roach whirl beneath

create explosive city life
        unleash truth of tune's title
                        Money Jungle:

        a life among millions
        constant skirmishes to make a living
        a world where survival
        is possible
        yet an eternal struggle

drums never cease
        bass sustains heartbeat sliding up and down
                and piano sings swings creates modern dance
                        of wild notes in cacophonous movement and sound
                                flings notes describing life's strife
                                      and illimitable fray

then all fades slowly
                into invisible night
                        bass and piano murmur a few last notes
                                final drumbeat slams door

between listeners and the mighty trio
        the impossible occurs as silence
                echoes into ache of nothingness

PREZ EXPLORES STARDUST

Lester Young's horn swells and dies, ebbs and flows;
his horn creates ocean waves defining warm late afternoon,
rising and falling, rising and falling on a quiet beach;

beneath his song Oscar Peterson and crew warm the land
where the water falls, and Young renews the blues
in a quiet way which breaks one's heart while Peterson

and Ray Brown create an undertow filled with life,
hope, and movement, until the Prez finishes and leads
listeners and musicians with a graceful glide deep into silence.

And the gloaming is once more upon us.

SAX AND SHAKESPEARE

What wind is this that rocks the room
in which I sit upon a rocker rolling
forth and back, book in hand, while Rollins'
sax roars with the might of surf's

explosion upon a beach besieged
by storm? And on the page which
I peruse, Lear rages, and engages
my heart and mind in ways I have never

known before. Such music -- sax
and Shakespeare overwhelm my mind
and heart, and the wind outside reminds
me of the truth they tell: all is fragile --

tree, bush, building, man, and beast, and I
rock, read, and listen, rock, read, and listen.

SOLEA

A trumpet cries over orchestral waves,
mourns like a wounded beast,
demands attention; orchestra swells,
trumpet riding its waves; silence;
then trumpet reappears softly in distance;
drums start a flamenco beat; horns quietly appear;
Miles' horn rises above the beat beneath; as it builds,
the horn mourns, the horn mourns, and drums beat;

the trumpet cries from the heart, from man's bones;
this is a funeral for mankind, for all life, lost, lost,
lost again and again; horn vanishes, and orchestra
lays a groundwork for the trumpet to reappear
and fade; drums continue, and trumpet dances in a wild
pageant of death; the orchestra remains together; the horn
sounds; pain, all pain, all kinds of pain, and the horn rises;
joined by the orchestra, the trumpet screams, disappears,

reappears in a rapid complaint above the muted orchestra;
the drums dance a wild dance; enter the orchestra swelling,
and the trumpet hangs high above in pure pain, pure emptying
of pain upon the earth, the dying earth, and the drums march on;
the orchestra rises; the trumpet weeps; the trumpet weeps,
and then rises above the marching orchestra, and the horn
dies in a wail seeping into the earth; the orchestra marches on;
then builds and builds, and the trumpet climbs, steps high above

filled with tears, filled with pain, filled with all mankind has lost;
as horn slips down into earth, the orchestra vanishes, save for drums'
steady martial dance; the trumpet returns, filled with all
of life's pain, all of life's losses; the orchestral dance
lays out beneath the horn's bleak plaint for all lost, all destroyed,
all no longer present to be loved; horn slips into earth; orchestra
whispers beneath purest song of Miles' horn, weeping horn, which slowly
slips into earth, the drums continuing a slow march to nothingness.

(for Miles Davis and Gil Evans)

ALL IS ONE, ONE IS ALL
   (for Ella Fitzgerald, Nina Simone, and Cleo Laine)

Trumpet and sax sail relaxed
above bobbing heads ensconced
in chairs of velvet comfort,
while bass thrums, and drums
rat-a-tat-tat in this or that rhythm;
the piano knows where the heart
swells and swells before dipping
and diving beneath surging waters
of fellow instruments, and all the audience

in heartfelt agreement lets emotion cascade
into the world, unleashed by musicians
and one singer who opens her heart to bleed
a balm to heal all who play, all who listen,
and to give full expression to a composer's
depth, breadth, sorrow, and hope of future beauty;
a worthwhile concert conjoins all present, stitches
trumpet, sax, bass, drum, piano, audience together;
all made one by a singer through whom life floods;

song has many wings, music fills many hearts;
the only impediments to descant, melody, euphonious joy,
is lack of imagination, arms folded in distrust;
concerts soar when all resound in unfettered unison;
certain women carry all our despair and express it
in unrestrained, full-throated carols of hope wed to pain;
leaving the concert, wind sighs through hair, bones,
and slow moving feet; music's range of beauty requires
attentive silence from all who witnessed its sacred rite.

SKETCHES

From a ninth story window,
a man watched ribbons of snow
twirl, swirl, and slowly embrace,
as they found a path to frozen
ground dimly lit by streetlamps
shivering in a cold wind; behind

him Miles Davis and Gil Evans'
orchestra were barely audible,
as they played the slow movement
from Rodrigo's Concierto de Aranjuez,
merging classical and jazz worlds,
as the snow outside merged death,

the inhuman, with a pure beauty
that took away the breath of the watcher,
as snow, wind, impersonal streetlamps,
frozen trees, and an occasional couple
drifting past hand in hand, created
a strange land of life, love, death,

and the inhuman, all filling one vast
impersonal canvas, and from the room
behind the watcher, the purest beauty
of sound flowed, indifferent to outside world;
from the watcher's eyes flowed one or two
tears; on street below one child stood, face

and arms lifted to sky, a wild smile curving
upwards, her arms flung above her head,
and her overcoat unbuttoned, windblown,
as night, snow, child, watcher, wind, and music
merged into a threnody mourning and celebrating
all there is, has been, might be, is lost, and can be found.

Tashkent, Uzbekistan, Winter 1998

MEMORY'S SALVATION

An old man ages,
his steps slow, hunger
for beauty increases,
as a river flows past
sweeping life with it;
slowly rocking, he revisits songs
in his mind, while his body fades:

Jussi Bjoerling sings "Amor Ti Vieta"
with pristine passion; The Little Sparrow
illuminates "Non, Je ne regrette rien"
with full-throated ardor; Lady Day
mesmerizes all who hear her "God
Bless the Child" with an offbeat
beauty no one else can duplicate;

and Jacques Brel sings "Marieke"
with an abandon few singers
can match; the old man rocks
slowly as a lifetime of music liberates
his mind from his decaying flesh,
and he hums along, often off-key,
but with a joyous melancholy.

The ancient imagines crossing the bar
accompanied by Handel's "Sarabande,"
then swept into an eternal ocean
by Coltrane's *A Love Supreme.*
The old fellow is convinced
that all beauty and meaning is best
expressed with the wonder of music.

EVENING AMBULATORY REVERIE

sheets of wind shake rattle and moan
through bushes trees and shrubbery

I lift my face into the blast and shift
my gait into a rolling stroll full

of sass vim vinegar and attitude
all due to wind swirling with vigor

of Sonny Rollins roaring with freedom
or the mighty Trane uplifting the world

with A Love Supreme and walls thrum
in the gale like drums unleashed by the might

of Elvin Jones the dead have risen in the world's
music and my aged limbs swing and sway

clumsy out of step but alive alive-o and I am
more alive than I have been in months

I find myself scat singing and ignore passersby
who stare I care only for the wind and its

bone-deep music music music and the rapidly
approaching gloaming which bears a fine mist

to sanctify the few out and about in wind rain
and oncoming night and its deep peace

IT WAS ALL SAX

arms of night enveloped me
pure sax singing in my ears
heart and caressing my mind
jazz all night long slow jazz
hot jazz dancing jazz and jazz

that slumbered that raised
and lowered blood pressure
love incarnate sweeping me
through long hours of darkness
all was sax sax sax and more sax

when day arrived and all grew still
and silent I rose to face a day
where roses grew and blossomed
everywhere I went and music
whispered at the back of my mind

DON'T FRET

Let's spend the night
sliding, gliding, striding
cross the floor.

Don't fret. The bass man
won't let our feet go astray.
Dip, swirl, and sway,

don't let this night get away
without a wild celebration
filled with ecstatic play

of body: legs, hips, chest,
feet, all awhirl, a-twirl,
all combine imagination

with rules of dance, and
liberation of music unleashing
wild hearts in courtship,

in dazzling exploration of time,
space, touch, arriving as one
at a perfect ending.

BILL EVANS PLAYS DANNY BOY

Rustle of fingers over piano keys
elicits whispers of grief, hope,
loss, and healing beauty. No lyrics,

but listeners know the words
and hear them in their heads,

as the piano traces an old tale
of parting, longing, loneliness,
and invests it with quiet passion,

sweeping listeners to a time lost,
yet present in heart and mind.

The music fades like a dying
breeze, and silence sheds tears
carried for years in memory.

AN EVENING JOURNEY

In early evening hush,
rain's soft susurration,
with a quiet elegance
one might find in a Bill Evans
or Lester Young or Miles Davis
solo, flows through open windows,
carries me from contemplation
into deep sleep where I float

downhill riding creek's current
through forests, past boulders,
into meadows where voices
of children echo, and distant past
welcomes me without question,
as certain songs or tunes
stir the heart whenever they
are sung or played,

such as "God Bless the Child,"
"Summertime," or "Stella by Starlight,"
and I drift through waves of music,
and the world laps against
my mind as it dozes, just as I drift
in and out of consciousness
when the rain carries me into memory,
then back to the edges of today.

A JAZZ THANKSGIVING OF A SORT

It was a rainy Thanksgiving when
everyone I was related to
or knew even somewhat
were out of town.

I found some semi-edible
turkey at Hughes Market, along
with frozen stuffing that proved
reasonably tasty, adequate

pumpkin pie slices, and discovered
leftover corn bread in my refrigerator.
I fumbled through jazz LPs and 45s in
a bin stashed against a wall and found

solace for a mournful afternoon: First,
Song for My Father. a fine upbeat
album by Horace Silver that led me
to beat my feet and play a drumbeat

on my dining room table while filling
my mouth with second hand food
from the supermarket; "Hang on Sloopy,"
the Ramsey Lewis jazz version of a pop hit,

had me bopping my head and scat singing
in my clumsy fashion; then Oscar Brown, Junior,
launched into his version of Nat Adderley's
"Work Song," and I was on my feet, singing along

at the top of my voice (not a problem as my
neighbors were all out of town), dancing,
stuffing my mouth with pumpkin pie, downing
rum and coke, and worrying my mutt, who found

a corner to curl up in. Some leftover turkey brought
her out of hiding. I put on Lou Rawls singing,
"Stormy Monday," just as the storm outside unleashed
lightning, thunder, and a wild windblown burst

of rain that shook the apartment. The timing made me
laugh and sing in harmony (of a sort) with Lou Rawls.
I picked up the little mutt and danced her around the room.
She tolerated the dance, as long as I fed her more scraps.

When I put her down, she retreated to her corner. I
finished my dinner serenade by playing a duet between
Ben Webster and Coleman Hawkins which led me to the couch
where I fell asleep, a pleasant ending to a solo Thanksgiving.

When I awoke, the wind was playing storm riffs outside my window,
rain was drumming on the building, and I embraced the darkness
with a grin, and a mumbled prayer of Thanksgiving. My hound climbed
onto the couch and curled up at my feet. My day was complete.

AND THEN THERE WERE NONE

Old man on a balcony
rocked his grief through
long afternoon, listened

to *Sketches of Spain*
hour upon hour, smoked
a pipe redolent of cloves,

an empty rocker next
to his draped with flowery
cushions, rocking from time

to time when wind chimed in.
He hummed trumpet solos
in broken raspy voice, recited lines

from King Lear with quiet passion
of Miles Davis or Bill Evans
at their melancholy best,

"O, thou'lt come no more.
Never never never never never."
He fell asleep while the music

played on, caught in a loop.
Miles welcomed onset of dusk.
Night spread its inevitable blanket.

PASSION FLOWER

After The Duke's quietly rippling, opening statement, such passion
in that flower as it opens to a world of unsuspecting listeners,
and Johnny Hodges sings in purest of alto sax voices a long limpid line,

elegantly phrased, a lovely horn grown flower of ineffable beauty
rising inevitably to bluest of deep blue skies, a musical flower
bestowing benediction on all within hearing, casually bequeathed,

with a look that suggests you don't truly understand what you are
being given, and the tone soars, then whispers, always pure, always
silky, always creamy, and the world for a few minutes grows more

beautiful, listeners float in a river of perfection, then all who hear
are diminished as all becomes once again ordinary, as the last perfect
note drops into silence, and Hodges disappears from behind the microphone,

and all is silence, all is routine, the quotidian coats life with blandness,
and all who heard the musical marvel that was Johnny Hodges play, pray
that memory will retain what was heard and bear witness that beauty can exist.

YOU DON'T KNOW WHAT LOVE IS

Trane's mighty horn gently nudges you, suggests
        you don't know what love is, elicits
                memory, sorrow, loss,

and the realization what once was
        will never again be,
                and tenderly Trane's sax

suggests loss can be transcended,
        but not without passing through grief,
                all healing rooted in fresh growth

replacing those years once rich in feeling,
        now empty, forlorn -- abandoned, lost, deprived;
                by tune's end Coltrane sails you to fresh growth,

where a tranquil future awaits, if you are brave enough to embrace it,
        embrace it,
                embrace.

GOING HOME

Tune of great beauty from Dvorak's
New World Symphony turned into folk song
sung with great passion and control by Paul Robeson,

embraced by Hank Jones and Charlie Haden,
turned into jazz hymn filled with loss, beauty, hope,
reminding one and all that music can contain pain,

almost unbearable pain, and (at the same time)
lift a listener to ecstatic heights that suggest
all is possible, all can be accomplished, and what is lost

can be found in memory, can be found Come Sunday,
can be discovered in the simplest and loveliest of tunes,
sung and swung effortlessly by classical, folk, and jazz musicians.

JOYFULLY BLUE

In the dark blue
deepening to black

of early evening,
I, silent and still, sit

listening to a gently rising
orchestra of sound:

a bird rhythmically sounding notes
which call to mind

Milt Jackson's mallets slow dancing
up and down a vibraphone, a chorale

of insects gradually growing louder, voices
of lads playing soccer in the distance

down a curving dirt road, men
and women talking, laughing, flirting,

and welcoming the deep peace of dusk's
warm and comforting waters;

I lean back and my eyes rest upon the rising
of a silvery moon, and I drift away.

            Kigali, Rwanda, September 2011

A PERFECT PARTNER

Such wonder exists in discovery
of love, as it drapes stone with finest cloth,
turns canned food into gourmet's delight,
lights bleakest night with golden moon
of fullest dimension, arrays sky
from side to side with wondrous displays
of stars in their wild beauty freed
from restraint, and unleashes deep in heart

and mind the purest beauty of "Round Midnight,"
swung and sung by Dexter Gordon and Junior Mance
in my memory, my everlasting memory that binds
the beauty of their sax and piano with every love
I have ever had and lost, had and sung goodbye
to, celebrated, whirled, twirled, and mourned,
as she vanished into rainy night or snowy afternoon,
and their music, their enchanted marriage with Monk's

off-beat, unique, musical depiction of perfection
keeps every true love forever present in my hoary
memory, remembrance, evocation found by stream,
river, mountainside, in sad sax, and dancing piano,
and all love is always present and always vanishing,
just like the notes found by musicians in snow-filled air,
creek, wind in trees, sweep of rain, and blessing
of a sun-filled afternoon shared with a perfect partner.

JOE WILLIAMS AT NEWPORT '63

"In the evening, in the evening, hey people, when the sun goes down,"
croons Joe Williams, "in the evening, hey people, when the sun goes down,
ain't it lonesome, ain't it lonesome, your baby's
not around, when the sun goes down."

Williams envelops the crowd with his smoky voice, as though they are all sitting
round a fire drinking, swaying to the music, as first Junior Mance's piano
makes the world swing, then Zoot Sims turns the world into amazing
tenor sax celebrating life, love, and beauty -- all are welcome, all are worthy;

ah, and now Howard McGhee makes his trumpet ring,
sing, and embrace the joys of life in a wild testament to love's truth;
followed by Big Joe who comes back in, builds to an amazing falsetto
that celebrates the sun going down, and sends one and all

out to find the one who is loved, needed, essential. As the music
fades to silence, the audience detonates into sustained applause.

SINKING INTO NIGHT

in evening western sky, golden clouds pile
beneath sinking crimson sun and spill
toward river and ocean with the beauty
and rhythmic precision of notes tumbling
from a vibraphone during a dazzling
improvisation by Milt Jackson

drops of falling color from the fading
evening sky spin the mind round and round
with the wild autoschediastic freedom
of sun tumbling into sea and the daring

song of Milt Jackson filling heart memory
and providing a path to a future

MILES AT WORK

Miles Davis convinced less is more
creates deeper feeling with fewer notes
than trumpet players thought conceivable
etches raw delicacy in fabric of air bends
time space fills them with sparse profundity

JUST LISTEN--IT IS EVERYWHERE

music can arrive without warning
on the breath of a passerby
a swirling tune afire
with hope or despair or peace

it can be a sound delicate as a butterfly's wings,
which slips through shuttered ears
and warms a cold center forever frozen
no more no more no more

tree bush and wind, children loose in a field,
lovers in the rain huddled together under
a rock outcropping, runner alone with miles
of footfalls and enveloping air,

all know in their bones the coming
of music, the promise of sound
to accompany creation's mighty dance
in all its manifold forms

ELEGANCE OF SIMPLICITY

the ripple of a midnight breeze
beneath warmth of a golden moon
the whisper of keys softly stroked
by Bill Evans or Duke Ellington
a kind mother comforting her child
life explored sotto voce
every gesture or hint of sound
a kind of prayer

OSCAR PETERSON TRIO + ONE

Some jazz albums bring city streets
alive in all their violence, danger, raw
excitement, threatening rhythms (think
Mingus or Sun Ra at their wildest);

other albums dive deep into the soul
of mankind in all its confusion, fear,
hope, or chart a musical path toward
salvation (think *A Love Supreme* or

Sketches of Spain). And then there
is the collaboration between Oscar
Peterson, Clark Terry, Ray Brown,
and Ed Thigpen, a joyous uninhibited

celebration of life by precise piano,
soaring trumpet and flugelhorn, wicked
gravelly mumbling voice, masterful
double bass, and supportive drums,

a collaboration that proclaims with
every note that life may be a wild ride,
but it is an exhilarating one, that each
and every bend in the road is a roller

coaster that cannot be anticipated,
but makes each passenger shout
Hallelujah, whether a note is high
or low, fast or slow, all is a musical

Thanksgiving, listening brings as much
fun for listeners, as performance did
for musicians. Even those who are crippled
let fingers and shoulders cut a rug.

A RATHER LARGE BLACKBIRD

came strutting, bouncing, hopping,
one might say winging it,
across the pavement
in front of an old motel.

With exaggerated bravado, the fellow
held his ground until the last second
before lifting off in raucous disgust
at an annoying Labrador pup

who bounded in merry pursuit. Heigh ho,
the vaudeville of everyday life.
An old fellow perched on a fountain's edge
provided a dance track on guitar to life's merriment.

(La Paz, Bolivia, June 2009)

ALONE ON A NIGHT STREET

Sailing through a midnight sky,
entangled in pine branches,
a golden full moon graces
the night with a beauty

comparable to a Bill Evans
or Duke Ellington solo,
nothing needed to expand
the floating vision;

the world is subtle, and repays
serious contemplation,
a lovely peace stripped
of life's angst and anger;

the simple act of breathing
in and out is a form of prayer.

IT WAS ALL ABOUT SAX

when man said the wind man
blowing when does the wind do
its voodoo upon leaf and bud

bloody the morning the storm
warning it is on its way its windy
winding wickedly roaring crack

thunder and snap way paving
the air for torrents for sheets waving
water across a landscape bare of movement

save the inexorable march of water
from hill crest to plains vanishing point
he blew harder his sax pumping sound and air

through the fair lands deluged with storm
with the wicked humor of broken notes rediscovered
in new keys the keys of life the keys of change

the keys to who and what I am you may be
maybe the keys to the kingdom of lusty life
he blew and vanished into the club's walls

and everyone left storming through the night
storming to the tunes reverberating in their heads
headed for home and a stormy night in a minor key

Tallinn, Estonia, Winter 2003

SOME STREET JAZZ

business men and women speed down main streets
all accelerating drums rhythm rhythm rhythm
no time for laid back strolling or casual contemplation

on side streets bass notes stutter step pause slip slide
side to side move on stopping turning left right left again
bebopping street hustlers and an audience out for a wild time

smooth glide of lovers navigating streets
without looking at any other than partners
sketched by quiet rippling piano keys

an obsessed teenager angry and confused
all his angst caught in sax's wild abandon
filled with swoops and dips and wild cries

and on a neighborhood stoop a trumpet solo mournful
full of doubt and hope and sweeping prayers leads into dusk
where so much is lost and so much is promised

as night deepens streets abandoned and house lights dim
piano sax trumpet bass and drums slowly fade
beneath a night wind rising throughout the city

LATE NIGHT TAPESTRY

midnight fast approaching
taxis jittering back and forth
across drunken lanes
of Saturday night city streets

a wannabe stud shouting out a window
at women in passing cars
god help him if one of them answers
he won't know what to do

a fraternity of drunks in full on
stagger mode down a rolling sidewalk
spewing laughter and vomit
hurling scatological comments wild and free

at any and all in their path
earning vituperative replies from many
while sending others who do not understand
late night streets' mythology scattering in dismay

there is a wild jazz here in the curly haired sax
player on the corner the fiddler outside
the movie theatre's midnight show the crazy drunk
spinning magical dance moves he could never do at noon

the hustler offering a chance to guess which card is which
as he switches them with the speed of a world class
drummer's hands as he lines his rap "which is which is which
ah wrong again try again come on odds say you'll win

sooner or later damn bad luck come back when you have
some more bread scratch moolah green stuff the means
to match your wits and eyes against my hands
my handle as good as the best point guards in the NBA"

even the cops are just more characters passing through
their badges visas to move freely in these parts
the real citizens of these streets acknowledge them
but know stray cats and dogs are more intrinsic to this world

this is a community where the herky jerky the unexpected the wild
blend with the smooth the elegant the lyrical the sensual the brutal
the violent to create a world that a modern day Bruegel would
immortalize as vital dangerous forever lit by streetlamps

BOIL'EM CABBAGE DOWN

Mark O'Connor and Wynton Marsalis erupt into a mighty sound
on fiddle and trumpet dancing round their musical playground
with a red hot band helping to boil'em cabbage down;

the tune leaps from fingers and lips with a red hot flame;
the notes have wings flying round the stage, every musician
engaged in a frenzy celebrating life with a gusto that flows

from trumpet, whirls from fiddle strings, is driven by rock steady
bass keeping their world in sync while a sax rips along beneath it all;
rhythm guitar, drums, and piano ripple and swirl

through whatever musical gullies need filling; every face is lit
with the purest joy, the audience claps and shouts, and their world
is intoxicated for six or seven minutes of musical frenzy;

when it ends, applause builds, everyone is standing, and all
know they have been blessed in ways that can't be anticipated.
Leaving, feet bounce on springs of remembered musical joy.

IN A DOWNTOWN DANCEHALL

Rollicking, rocking, roaring denizens of the dance floor
freestyle wild flips, turns, leaps, splits, astonishing
feats of ingenuity that shape movement sans limitation,
as some long forgotten swing band blazes over the speakers,
and those on the sidelines shout encouragement
and occasional suggestions; feet glide, slide, skip, boot,
scoot, and boogie all round the hall; arms wave overhead,
drop down to sides as fingers wiggle, hips swing and sway,
and all of day's worries and confusion slips away
in the holy fury of bodies liberated in exuberant exploration
of space, time, movement, and unfettered imagination.

MUSICAL ALCHEMY

Man on bass has left the room,
his fingers
still dance along strings.

NAT KING COLE

croons "Chestnuts Roasting on an Open Fire;"
voice velvety as cocoa butter
warms listeners, seats them round a hearth;

every word, every idea, clear as a bell,
envelop listeners, rhythmically rock them,
invite smiles, affection, communal celebration.

As the final note fades, silence settles,
a silence in which a few still sway
in memory and in hope for a better day.

NEWS COMES OF YOUR DEMISE
(for Ben Saltman, 1927-1999)

A picture, a poem, a book,
a few anecdotes, a foolish
argument barely remembered,

a dinner where we saved
the world from fools
much like us, these few

things are all I carry with me,
and I grieve that so little
remains of one who meant

so much for so long;
in restaurant where I sit
staring at your wife's letter,

an old jukebox plays "So What"
from *Kind of Blue*, in a room filled
with expats from a dozen nations,

and I remember our discussions
of relative merits of Miles versus
Trane, Ellington versus Basie,

Lady Day versus Ella,
and all those thousands of words
now seem inane; only the music matters,

as only the life mattered;
I pray we did not waste both,
and the music continues to fill

the small cafe in Tashkent
where I grieve, thousands of miles
and a dozen years from home.

Dolor fills the horns of Trane,
Miles, and Cannonball, music that mourns
life's limitations yet eases my distress.

I sip a Benedictine and Brandy, eavesdrop
on conversations in multiple languages,
understand nothing but irreparable loss.

(Tashkent, Uzbekistan, 1999)

OF FIREFLIES JAZZ AND LOST RELATIVES

In the gloaming's last embers, a swirl of fireflies
flits, flashing brief bursts of light, as certain
trumpet and sax players will play swift staccato
notes, each one perfect, lighting the minds,
imaginations, and hearts of listeners who
have no idea how such perfection is achieved,

knowing only that life will never be this perfect
again, just as the children chasing the fireflies
will never again be so filled with joy, as this
moment when time stops and all is wild surmise
about this moment and the next and the next;
the perfection of visual and sonic beauty remains

forever beyond understanding, no matter how many
tomes seek to explain; yet heart, mind, memory,
and imagination embrace both with the fervor
with which we cling to the debris left by a departed parent.
Somehow when I remember fireflies, departed musical
geniuses, and vanished friends and relatives, I hear

the anguished beauty of Miles Davis navigating the heartrending
currents of Concierto de Aranjuez, as fireflies navigate
evening breezes, as great horn players fly, float, and dance
with ease through difficult passages, and we, one and all,
are blown here and there, always seeking beauty and its
ineffable pain, peace, and liberation from self.

TWO WHO HAVE SEEN BETTER DAYS

Exuberant rain dances on a spring window
in concert with Ramsey Lewis unleashing
"Hang on Sloopy" on the radio;

who would have thought it possible
piano, rain, and wind might lift an old man
to his feet in an aging parody of a jig;

the septuagenarian's ragged voice belts out
those words that can be remembered while
the visitor in the room, an old friend unseen

for years, sings along, misses as many words
as his host in a wild unanticipated toast to life;
neither of these old scoundrels are fit to dance,

much less sing, but both give it all they got, as wind
rises and falls, as rain sweeps away lost and lonely years,
as life flowers in the most unlikely of crucibles.

SUDDENLY ON A BACKSTREET

A trumpet from a nearby building soars
with wild brilliance of tone, swoops
down, down, down into lowest reaches
of its range, dances higher once again
in a playful pattern of two steps higher,

one lower, two more up the staircase,
then veers into wild leaps, bounding
throughout the range of trumpet
possibilities, the tone pure, harsh,
guttural, celebratory, grieving,

notes slow, soft, barely audible, then
blaring, rising higher and higher with unfettered
volume and passion; finally, the music
stops mid-note; looking up, I discover a man
of indeterminate age in a ragged plaid shirt,

horn in hand, in a window three stories
above me, eyes lost in the distance, face pressed
against panes, wearing an expression of loss,
as he watches a troupe of lads shouting
and laughing in a celebration of youth's freedom.

As I walk away, I hear the tears of a Harmon mute,
barely audible, whispering "Round Midnight."
I glance behind me to discover the trumpeter
has opened his window to bestow his song
upon barren streets as shadows envelop his world.

ILLINOIS JACQUET

(in response to an invitation
musical and raucous from the fingers
of Wild Bill Davis tickling the keys
of his organ seeking a musical response
by someone and something of equal stature)

Illinois I say accepted the challenge and blew
some blue some very blue blue blue notes
that set listeners nodding heads
moving shoulders slowly to the pain
contained within each swinging phrase

feet shuffled bodies swung a slow dance
back and forth listeners acknowledging
Jacquet's testimony etched in raw sustained
pain pain pain that drew moans
from the depths of all who heard

such beauty from the heart and mind
of Illinois doing musical forensics
on his soul until a long sustained rising note
drew Wild Bill Davis to unleash
his waiting organ into wailing conversation

with sax and drum in unfettered collaboration
which led to an ending that lifted listeners
to their feet in sustained shouts applause
and joy joy joy at what had just been heard
oh me oh my souls must fly on certain days

JOHN LEE HOOKER

cooks some "Blues for Christmas."
They mourn life's vicissitudes, yet
listeners tap feet, swing, sway,
slow rock shoulders, hips, and legs;

as the guitar charts a course through life,
the drummer lays out a beat that even
an old man can follow; the sax wails
a tale of heartbreak to make listeners know

they are not alone, while the piano
slips in comments that make a listener
smile and nod his head. Brother Hooker's voice
is worn, torn, essential to discovery of joy.

JUST OUT FOR A WALK
(for Joseph Glaser and Robert Fox)

downtown small town backstreets
gimping along, walking stick in hand,
my feet beat the street like a drummer

always just behind the beat and all
around me folk create their own music
an old woman on a corner scolding

herself in staccato bursts of sound
Coltrane would have recognized
three wee bairns skip rope and chant

in rhythms Horace Silver might
have included in his best work
a lad bops swiftly through a nearby

intersection with the funky
lightning quick deftness of the mighty
Charlie Parker dancing through a solo

his groove moving at the speed of light
leaning against a wall with the weight
of years and the world two old men

quietly talk talk and talk mixing smiles
and soulful nods as they shake heads
at all they've seen and known both

kind of blue conversation sailing
wherever memory and imagination
take them sharing riffs that fit

90

together with the perfection
of Miles musically chatting
with Cannonball and Trane

and I suddenly realize all life
is music harmonious dissonant
free-flowing stuttering full-throated

whispered celebratory or grief-stricken
all contain melody rhythm (heart)beat
memory and imagination

LIFE'S MUSIC

Arturo Sandoval's trumpet mourns "The Windmills of Your Mind"
on a stereo, notes floating to the street below where an aged couple
of sixty or so slowly glide arm in arm through an early spring evening
that is livened by a cool breeze blowing her hair across his grizzled beard,
as they lightly rest head against head and smile at the elegiac music
that sings of what was and was lost, what might have been and wasn't,
while they have overcome and live in quiet joy at what is and will be,
each day a duet of memory, hope, loss redeemed, and love that endures.

MEDITATION WHILE LISTENING TO SOME LATIN JAZZ

swing swagger and sway
she bop she bop drift those feet
first one way then another
swirl round and round and back again
light up the floor fly up above
the chandeliers up where the music
wanders on its way into memory

where music's invention of time
is lost refound soars on imagination's
wings into memory's timeless space
where all is now and all is lost and all
is gained and all the costs of living
are stored in a personal inventory open
only to the self shuffling through life

down a long constantly shifting path
adrift toward whatever awaits
and meantime we dance to all the music
life creates one hopeful despairing
daring step after another as we laugh
cry sing and stutter step through
our winding spiraling days

SOLO DANCE TO BLUES

a girl dances alone in a room
to an old blues tune sung
on a boom box by Mance Lipscomb

she whirls leaps and floats
on her toes with eyes shut
head laid back on an air cushion

an effortless whirlwind in a space
shared only with a funky slide guitar
and roughhewn marvelous voice

carving sound into pain intense and casually revealed
the singer states Joe Turner Killed a Man
the dancer wilts like a dying flower

then brings the man and her dance back to life
wild utterly free life and the guitar and voice
slice a listener's heart into a slow beat beat beat

IN MEMORY OF TWO CROONERS

Let's hear it for Bing and Frank
(before he was chairman of the board).
Their smooth crooning

set crowds on fire, made young girls swoon,
ignited bodies and souls
to swing and sway, and generated

memories (that lasted for decades)
for an up and coming generation,
as they redefined popular music,

intertwined it with jazz,
broke boundaries between audiences
and performers, set an era

aflame dancing fast and slow, and helped
turn a bland world hip, established
it is never too soon for anyone to croon.

AIN'T IT THE TRUTH

choirs of insects serenade night
couples bury faces in lovers' hair
distant train's cry soars through dark
town settles into silence
one face peers through half-opened window
seeking a single light

as Mose Allison sings in the background
"Your mind is on vacation, but your mouth
is working overtime"
story of my life thinks the listener
wishing there was someone available
to share his "overtime"

Allison launches into
"Seventh Son of a Seventh Son"
auditor mutters I should be so lucky
trashes his whiskey bottle
collapses on the couch
slips into muted snores

POWER OF A JUKE

A lad fired up a jukebox; his feet
spun left, then right; he lured a lass
into his arms; their feet caught fire;

they scorched the floor from one side
of the room to another; suddenly, left,
right, and center, the room had an ecstatic

herd of teenagers whose fleet feet
scalded the boards all through the room,
and the night came alive with joy's

magnetic bonfire; hallelujah, brother
and sister, let us praise life in all its many,
exuberant, illimitable characteristics.

On the box, sax, trumpet, piano, bass, and drums
swung, swung, and swung, until all were done:
lads, lasses, and magic players igniting instruments.

WHISPERS OF THE HEART

My mother, voice colored by the hint of Virginia
even after decades away, softly talks of years past,
friends, parents, deceased spouse, siblings,
all lost to mortal frailty, swallowed by time.

Her monologue has the gentle beauty of a solo
by Bill Evans at his most introspective. His musings
deftly drawn on a keyboard and her murmurs
to listening sons are as one, quiet music that soars.

It sometimes seems that all life, whether muted or lived
with abandon, is an elegy for time's relentless movement,
whether past, present, or future. No matter how restrained
or uninhibited, life expresses whispers of the heart.

THEY ALL INHABIT THE NIGHT

all night I dreamed I was lost
at sea in an alley on a battlefield
in a junkyard in a waterfront dive

when suddenly I found a room
filled with music where fear
was eased where losses were mourned

where hope was discovered where
horns and voices and rippling piano
blessed all who listened as a rainstorm

washed streets and buildings as lightning
flashed and thunder roared and music
blended in perfect harmony and suddenly

I recognized those who filled my dream
oh Ella whose scat singing sweeps away
all pain ah Lady Day who absorbs all grief

in your broken voice while Lester's sax
soothes your heartbreak damn my eyes
and ears Coleman's raw power matches

Joe Williams' unfettered exuberance
note for note and the mighty Miles Trane
Cannonball collaboration makes a dreamer

(continued on next page)

kind of blue and thoroughly blessed
while Dizzy and Bird reinvent
music's possibilities and I sing along

in my dream with wild abandon
pure sound with no words needed
until I wake with song fading

from my head yet buried in my heart
heirlooms of music I will never lose
as long as their magic names resound

IT WAS A COLD AND RAINY NIGHT

The old man in the backstreet dive
played a slow blues on his battered guitar,
a funky lament for lost years, opportunities

for love squandered, dreams vanished
into canyons of memory, each note

fragile, yet an astonishing mixture
of loss, pain, and unexpected joy
that his hands and heart could still

produce such sorrowful beauty.
Some kid, in his late teens, wandered in,

opened up a case, and pulled out
an heirloom guitar that must have been
as old as the lad's grandfather.

Neither spoke to the other, but the new
arrival began to lay in a surprisingly skilled

rhythm background. No one in the bar
paid much attention as the two on
the tiny stage created a world of their own.

Gradually, the old man took his guitar
to places few could follow, but the kid

hung with him, note for note, then began
to create harmonies that jumped from above
to below the old man's notes and then back

up again. The ancient's lips sketched the ghost
of a smile; he began to play faster,

wilder, investigating terrain he had not
visited in years. The youngster followed,
his guitar dancing around the wildfire

created by the other. The audience grew
silent, still, began to listen carefully.

Both guitars played ever more slowly,
sorrowfully, quietly, until the old man
hit a note that hung and hung in the air;

there was silence for a few seconds
before the kid took the last note, sent it

soaring higher, higher, higher, then
dropped it lower and lower, like a leaf
swirling through autumn air, and a final

note hung suspended. The reverberation
seemed to last forever, then silence fell.

No one moved or spoke as the two onstage packed up
and slowly walked out the door, disappeared
in different directions into cold wet night.

LATE SPRING RAIN

swollen with spring rain
creek sings in crooked path round
boulders trees down mountainside

a song wild as Coltrane solo
or Mingus big band creation
wind accompanies water

with utter abandon of flute
sax trumpet and mad drummer
who recognize no rules

all is possible all is true
all can be achieved
as the water knows

no limitations no boundaries
so jazz defines exploration
its wild freedom makes its own rules

ADRIFT IN EVENING

twilight fades with grace and elegance
of muted trumpet solo's last notes

drifting into memory   for example
the evanescent sorrow of notes
blown by Miles Davis using a Harmon

mute where the final sounds are
a mere whisper yet contain a lifetime

of grief hope and wistful surmise
so too evening's last wisps of light
contain long departed ocean voyages

athletic and academic feats now
barely credible and vanished lovers

a hint of their smiles the sound
of their voices in night's solitude
caught in last echoes of birdsong

and the lost beauty left behind by Clark Terry
Dizzy Gillespie and Miles always Miles Davis

JOYOUS EVENING WITH THE BLUES

Dexter Gordon blew blue
blue notes for hours in his visit
to my CD player,

accompanied by wicked syncopations
rapped on window and roof
by bursts of rain as it came and went

and returned again, as Mr. Gordon
and the Junior Mance Trio entranced
Montreux back in 1970, along

with me and my two friends
silently nodding in (more or less) time
to music from over forty-five years ago

and icy rain in the here and now;
we spent time consuming "Fried Bananas,"
dreaming of a "Sophisticated Lady,"

bouncing and dancing in chairs and on sofa
to "Rhythm-a-Ning," slow swaying
to "Body and Soul," tears in our eyes,

rediscovering the essence of the blues
in "Blue Monk," and bopping out
freely and wildly around the room

(continued on next page)

in response to "The Panther."
When the CD concert ended, we all
smiled and silently went our various ways,

and the rain continued a slow serenade,
as if it too had been taken on a journey
that led to a joyous copious weeping.

FRIDAY NIGHT DELIGHT

Twang of a bottleneck guitar sings into neon night;
swings bodies aching to dance up, down, and around,
time after time after time in a whirling world where bodies

rhyme; legs glued to legs, hips to hips, and lips to lips;
guitar's ringing invitation to take flight lingers in heavy
humidity like a final sip of sweet, bitter lemonade enticing

drinker to take one more taste, just one; and a crazy pianist
blazes up and down a keyboard, an alto sax sets fire
to the heavy air in the crammed club with sawdust

covering the floor, just one dropped match away
from a conflagration, a word that captures the blues
trio who ignite every person in the joint into a burning,

blazing mass that jumps, jives, and dives with wild
uninhibited movement, movement one step away from collapse,
from making love, from taking flight into a new world and time.

SOME EMBRACE A MIGHTY STORM AND PRAY FOR WINGS TO FLY

Ah, the splendid raging of early autumn rain
on abandoned fields still embracing thigh-high
grass not yet yellowed and dying,

while the river flows (as ever) mightily down
to a waiting ocean, and certain old men limping
with a wet joy down back streets and dirt lanes

sing songs they've known since childhood, as they
clumsily execute a dance step here or there,
and a few children escaped from classrooms

race along soaked railroad tracks with all available
speed, daring one another to flip, flop, fly,
and do walking handstands down abandoned rails.

As early evening envelops landscape, one by one,
the young and old fade into homes, trailers, and other
shelters scattered here and there, until only a small

handful of shadows populate the wet landscape
which has been largely abandoned to cloud, rain,
and a half-moon cradled in pale clouds sweeping

over forest, empty fields, and arrival of lightning's
fierce scrawl from one side of sky to another,
accompanied by crash of thunder's tympani.

The few who remain outside in storm
and blanketing night sing hallelujah in their
lonely hearts and pray for wings to fly.

HOSANNAH TO THE MUSIC OF THE STREETS

the streets, midnight streets
        drunks, lovers, searchers, dreamers,
    wild men and women, the young hunting
what it is to be
                a man or a woman, older folk
        who want to be young again, the crazy,
the mentally lame, the physically impaired, those
        who are willing to dare any and everything
                the body and mind can attempt,
the watchers, the doers, the fools, the saints,
        those who have never achieved, those
who can no longer achieve, those who try and fail,
those who try and get partway to their goal, those
        who rise high above all while knowing this cannot
                last, will not last, but for now they
                are flying far above what even they
        have imagined, all of these people of the night,
of the world abandoned by the straight, the clean, the pure,
the abiders of rule and law and expectation, this night world
lives in the raw sound of Rollins, Coltrane, the Hawk, the soaring
Bird, the cool pain of Miles, the hard bop of Horace Silver,
the idiosyncratic genius of Monk and Mingus who see and hear
what we don't, and create sound and rhythm that bemuses and dumbfounds,
exalts and delights, all this and so much more, both explore the night world
        which few understand, many roam, investigate, and embrace,
                and only the deep blue jazz hearts of the greatest musicians
can bring alive, articulate, make the great and the small celebrate,
and turn music into prayer, into psalms of the spirit and the flesh,
give me an amen and dive beneath
                the surface of music's sound, fury, and holiest of blessings

BIOGRAPHY

Michael L. Newell was born in Florida in 1945. In addition to living in thirteen states, he has lived in Japan, The Philippine Islands, Thailand, The United Arab Emirates, Jordan, Kuwait, Uzbekistan, Mexico, Egypt, Estonia, Saudi Arabia, Bolivia, and Rwanda. He currently lives in a small town on the Florida coast.

Newell studied writing with Benjamin Saltman and Ann Stanford. His poems have appeared in a number of periodicals including *Aethlon: The Journal of Sport Literature*; *Bellowing Ark*; *College English*; *Current*; *English Journal*; *First Class*; *The Iconoclast*; *Issa's Untidy Hut*; *Jerry Jazz Musician*; *Lilliput Review*; *Poetry Depth Quarterly*; *Poetry/LA*; *Rattle*; *Shemom*; *Ship of Fools*; *Tulane Review*; and *Verse-Virtual*.

Some of Newell's previous books include *A Stranger to the Land*; *The Long Gores Suite*; *Seeking Shelter*; *A Long Time Traveling*; *Collision Course*; *Traveling without Compass or Map*; *Meditation of an Old Man Standing on a Bridge*; *Wandering*; *Each Step a Discovery*; *Diddley-Bop-She-Bop*; *Making My Peace*; *The Harry Poems*; and *Still the World Beckons: New and Selected Poems*.

COMMENTS ON JAZZ POEMS BY MICHAEL L. NEWELL

Michael Newell's jazz poems reveal the poet's deep appreciation for this most American of musical forms. The poems display an underlying musicality and a sharp insight into the artists and their myriad backgrounds. Whether he is describing the musicians, a smoky venue, or bodies swaying, the reader can hear the music and feel the motion. Settle down in a comfortable chair, read these poems, and play some cool jazz. Even with the volume turned down low, you won't be able to resist tapping your feet as you read or jumping up and dancing to Newell's seductive beat.

-- Michael Minassian, author of *Time is Not a River* and *Morning Calm*

If you know little about jazz or poetry, this book will be full of profit and delight. It will teach you about the history of the most American of music, its giants, feeling and craft. If you know about jazz and poetry, you'll see at once how marvelously Michael L. Newell has matched his knowledge and love for the former with his gift for the latter. Here are the heroes with their tragedies and talent. Here are evocations of their sublimity and pain. Newell does more than celebrate the improvisations, rhythms, and moods of the music; he reproduces them in lively, moving, and inspired verse. These poems about jazz are jazz poems.

Robert Wexelblatt, Author of *Hsi-wei Tales, Girl Asleep and Other Poems*, etc.

Whether riffing with rhythms or playing with tone while describing rain's quiet drizzle or a voice shredded by cigarettes, Michael L. Newell's jazz poems immerse readers in their expansive quality. Newell is deeply passionate about jazz and like good jazz, Newell's poems embody a wide spectrum of emotions and moods. Imbued with a deep and humble awareness, these poems are able to carry readers to the boundary of what words can name before music extends their expression. Read them and be touched with a recognition of our common humanity.

Anna Citrino, author of *A Space Between*

Michael L. Newell's jazz poems add to one's appreciation for jazz. He writes about both famous and less well-known jazz musicians, interacts with the music in a deeply personal way, and challenges a reader to embrace the music. He invites readers to join him in a love of jazz in its many forms. His poetry, like jazz, covers decades. In recent years, his poems have frequently appeared in the pages of my magazine.

-- Joe Maita, Editor/Publisher/Founder of *Jerry Jazz Musician*.

www.ingramcontent.com/pod-product-compliance
Lightning Source LLC
La Vergne TN
LVHW091550170726
843492LV00007B/2126